Winter Morning with Crow

Akron Series in Poetry

Winner of the 1996 Akron Poetry Prize

Winter Morning with Crow

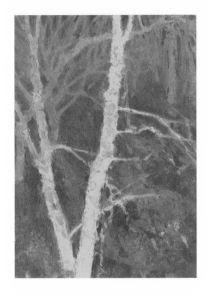

Clare Rossini

The University of Akron Press
Akron, Ohio

Thanks to the editors of the following publications for permission to reprint these poems, which originally appeared in their pages (sometimes in slightly different versions): *The Antioch Review:* "The Good Fortune of Others"; *Black Warrior Review:* "Leave of Absence"; *Boston Women's Art Collective Newsletter:* "The Painter Goes Fishing"; *The Dickinson Review:* "After the Old Testament Lecture, Taking the Shortcut Home," "Summering in the Midwest," and "The Lighthouses Are Automated"; *The Iowa Journal of Literary Studies:* "Fra Angelico's *Annunciation,* Convent of San Marco"; *Italiana Americana:* "Final Love Note"; *The Kenyon Review:* "'Life Before Birth,' a Display," "A Mourning Dove in New York City," and "Self-Portrait as Woman Posed on Flowered Couch"; *New England Review:* "Nightmare"; *Poet Lore:* "The Young Men of Division Street"; *Poetry:* "An Imaginary Tapestry" (formerly titled "Ideology") and "Valediction"; *Poetry Northwest:* "For a Friend Since Youth"; *Prairie Schooner:* "The Pleasures of Perspective"; *The Sycamore Review:* "Still Life with Pear."

"Valediction" appeared in the 1996–97 *Anthology of Magazine Verse and Yearbook of American Poetry* (Palm Springs, CA: Monitor Press, 1997) as well as in *The Best American Poetry 1997* (New York: Scribner, 1997); "Elegy in Four Parts" appeared in *Our Stories of Miscarriage* (Minneapolis: Fairview Press, 1997); "Curriculum Vitae," "Calla Lily Studies, Nos. 1–12," "Nightmare," "The Good Fortune of Others," and "Among Cows" were printed as broadsides in an art-book edition titled *Selections from the Claudia Poems,* which was produced by book artists Mary Hark and Mary Jo Pauley (Minneapolis: Minnesota Center for the Book Arts, 1994). "A Mourning Dove in New York City," "For a Friend Since Youth," "Self-Portrait as Woman Posed on Flowered Couch," "The Pleasures of Perspective," and "Leave of Absence" appeared in *Plain Songs* (Northfield: Carleton College, 1990).

Thanks to Carleton College and the Monastery of St. Benedict; MacDowell Colony, Yaddo Corporation, and the Vermont Studio Center; and the Minnesota State Arts Board, all of which generously supported the writing of these poems. Thanks also to my readers over the years: Robin Behn, Joseph Byrne, Jeff Friedman, Frederick Kettering, Susan Jaret McKinstry, Elizabeth Macklin, John Ramsay, Bob Tisdale, and Chico Zimmerman. Special thanks to Christina Templeton as well as to Lorie Tuma for her administrative assistance.

Thanks to Diana Postlethwaite for the title of "Mortal Thoughts."

All inquiries and permissions requests should be addressed to the Publisher, The University of Akron Press, 374B Bierce Library, Akron, Ohio 44325-1703.

Rossini, Clare.
    Winter morning with crow / Clare Rossini. — 1st ed.
      p. cm. — (Akron series in poetry)
    ISBN 1-884836-30-5. — ISBN 1-884836-31-3 (pbk.)
    I. Title. II. Series.
  PS3568.O84725W56   1997
  811'.54—dc21   97–15080
                                                                CIP

Manufactured in the United States of America

Second printing, 1998

For Joseph

Contents

III. Leave of Absence

Knowledge of a man is different from knowledge
of a lyre. —*Plato*

The point of vision and desire are the same.
—*Wallace Stevens*

I go walking after midnight searching for You.
—*Patsy Cline*

I. First Snow

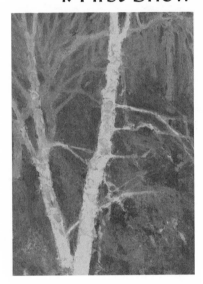

"Life Before Birth," A Display
(The Chicago Museum of Science and Industry)

The first was curled and so small
It shone like a remote star
Caught in the crossed bars of museum lights.

The next was something like a fish,
The sign said; the one after it,
A fetal bird budding wings.

I stalled before the one which seemed
Irremediably human,
The arms elongated, erupting into hands,

The head lolling over the chest
Whose ribs branched delicately
Behind flesh shining like unlit wax.

I stood before it, amazed
That I had been star, fish, bird,
Then this impeccable sleeper—

While beneath the pastels
Of my stiff new Easter dress,
My bones nosed out in new directions,

My cells flared up, melding an architecture
Whose final shape would be forged
In the foundries of desire.

Half-Price Suite at the Park Central

Who cares if the paintings on the walls are prints,
At a secondhand remove
From the genius whose vision they borrow?
Or that the fan in the bathroom rattles
As it whirls away our mist?

We've never had a room this high, never
Thrown cash away to get this close to the clouds.
They're our vacuous siblings now.
We assess their fluffiness and grays,
How they part to let the sun stream forth—

The sun, our competitor in height.
We pull the shade. Sleep through the afternoon,
Then order in Chinese, a minor festival
Of sticks, steam, and paper boxes.
Our fortunes are good. Our fortunes
Predict my laugh, our kiss. And then the king-sized bed
Consumes our consummation.

You sleep. I stand at the window, alone
With the Sheraton's big red S
Glowing from a crowd of dusky midtown towers.

The cries of taxi horns float up, the same two notes
Over and over. It's a wounded song,
And it makes me ache
For the works and days of my own kind,
Those mortal fools at street level.

Summering in the Midwest

As one who knows the sea in the old sense
Of the verb, having felt its reckless waves
Probe me deeply before moving on
In the machismo way of water;

Having dozed beyond its savvy glitter
And wakened to find it impatiently
Crashing a few feet from my exhaustion;
Having gone home, still rocking internally;

I suspect these nicely squared-off counties,
Their empty silos ready to receive
September's wheat, their clouds lingering
Over the fields, as if with tenderness.

These are not my metaphors. Instead,
The wave's dreamy crescendo, the stalled depths,
The rabid and seasonless pounding.
And the undertow, proposing formlessness.

The Painter Goes Fishing

When the tip at the end of your rod
Scribbles frantically on the air,

When that whole length of nervous fiberglass
Bends to the blankness of water,
Beseeching it,

You struggle to your feet, most in love
With this business now,
When it first comes into view—

That mute metallic shape
Wending its way up toward you
Through the wavering fields of water,

Now,
When it could be fish
Or angel, you don't know, you've just come
To an unmarked place in readiness—

You, standing now, straining to hold
Your violent rod,
Like Abraham to his God, crying out,
Here I am!
As the surface breaks in a shower of light.

You Left Me to This House

The roof is wanting. It can't take sun anymore, or rain,
Which drops free-fall through the attic,
Seeps through the bedroom ceiling,
And plunks on my head. I waken,
My pillow, my pillowed head damp.

The basement sours. It's moisture-rich,
A brick's width from bald dirt,
Indelicate as a groin. Wiring is stapled to the rafters
Like nerves, runs excitedly all over.

My life is raised
On this barbarian foundation
With a furnace at its core.
Last week, I threw the door open:
Fire! They took me aback, those red flames beating all night
On old red metal. While one floor up,
My walls crack—

What anger are they getting out?
The fault lines flicker
Up and down the stairwell. The carpenter says
They are caused by moisture:
I need vents, I need insulation. But all my needs
Are on the surface,

And as I read at night, something thumps
In the wall behind me, then makes
Low plaintive sounds. How did it get in, this desperation
Shuffling against plaster? It's the last unslaked
Thirst of summer, so close
That I can feel its breath. Like your breath on me. Your breath.
You.

Vision and Prayer

This morning
When I woke at six,
The terrace fence still enclosed
A square of night.

But the sky above it
Was so beatified with blue
That it might have been done
By Angelico.

At that moment,
My unconscious off-guard,
Bright and close
To the surface,

I did not think
But *knew* that you were
In or of that sky,
Looking down with the calmness

I've seen in your eyes
As your hand
Slowly
Brings my body to fire.

The mind
Is my brother and keeper,
I know. The mind
Counts and stacks,

Moves beyond the body's
Centrifuge of heat
To set up house
In havens of the past,

Of God-Is-With-Us,
Of future kisses,
Apocalypses,
Reckonings.

But when I am with you,
I want nothing but your occasion,
The present that
Fails and fails:

What more do I need,
When, at your site,
I find all the grief that the heart
Knows it must know?

Oh God-
Who-May-Be-With-Us,
Sign me up
For the feast of faith,

The truth of truths invisible,
Anything to drag me above
This carnal address
Where love,

Like the fickle bird of my elm,
Sings some nights
And some nights leaves me
To the roost of silence.

How to Tempt a Fish

(with counsel from Buddha's *Dhammapada*)

Go when the sun's pink shafts
First impale the horizon, rowing until you tire,
Until the tatters of mist clear. You will find yourself
In the middle of a wide, round kingdom of wavelets.

     "All is transient." When one sees this, he is above sorrow.

It's not easy to gut the worm's thick, ribbed life,
That fidgeting residue of last night's rainstorm
Found on the sidewalk between your
Powder-blue cottage and the canteen.

Throw it over, this hook
In worm's clothing. Watch it drop, your invitation
To whatever hunger resides down there
Where lake-weeds waver and light
Goes milky and errant.

     "All is sorrow." When one sees this, he is above sorrow.

Sip your coffee, tepid now.

Watch dragonflies knit up and down together, their wings
Puréed by motion.

Consider the bobber, riding the waves
As jazz rides the underground beat of its measures.

Minutes or hours pass—who's counting?

     "All is unreal." When one sees this, he is above sorrow.

Remember, the pleasure's not in the catch,
The sunfish dangling boatside, twitching drops
Of water and blood.

The pleasure's in the temptation:
Living simply, in a boat-shaped room,
Your desire fixed on nothing
But the absent, ravishing hook.

From Abstinence, N.H.

There's a hill at the end of every street here,
For closure. The sun does its business
Discreetly behind them, that blood-red business
At the end of day. All I see is pink sky,
Fading. Then the night birds do their murmur thing.

No, I'm not sad to have left the plains behind.
They straddled too much space. Voices got lost
In them, lives could. Mine did for awhile.
Then I found it by the smoke going up,
The closeted flame.

              These hills are not mountains:
Let's get that straight. Mountains impose. Hills
Merely limit the possible. I'm safe
In the shade they constuct. I haven't made it
To the top of one but once, in the fall.
What a view! Hill after hill, in yellow, pink.
(The leaves here are famous.) And far off, dreamlike,
A peak capped with snow . . .

              It's good to know your place.
How could I, back there, where the horizon line
Went on and on beneath unfettered clouds,
Completely visible to the eye
And shameless as Manet's *Olympia*?

There are primal forces here, don't get me wrong.
Broken-down stone walls. Back-pasture goats.
And something emotes in the woods, I've heard it
At night, I've felt it pass over my face,
A light mouth—

God knows what I would do
If I went back, or whether I'd unpack
That secondhand silk robe I wore one night.
The color wasn't bad. The evening light there
Went on past seven: that was nice. And the birds
Didn't sound sad, as they do here, where I live
In a valley near a small brick church.
I read good books. I go to bed early.

Final Love Note

For months we've been together, hardly wanton,
Never touching. Yet your shade commingled
With my clothes strewn on the floor, and your wind
Moaned over me at night, never tiring
As human lovers do. My lifted garden,
Pure-green, wooden-hearted, all your leaves moved
Summer-long, then suddenly caught fire.
In winter I endured your silences,
My sight tangled in your black network
Which trapped whatever moon was on the rise.

This summer, the slugs ate the yellow hearts
Right out of my lilies, while you, elm, died on—

Dying as you have for years, leafless branches
Subdividing your shade. Slowly the sun
Found more of my roof, the attic grew hotter.
Some nights, the heat would not leave my bed
Until two or three, while I tossed and turned
In my abandonment.

                                This morning,
I hear the chain saw cry out ecstatically.
My heart beats. Then a dull thunder shakes the house.

Your many arms are falling. And I must live
More with sky now, that garish blue stretch
Or drafty ceiling harshly lit by stars.

To Mount Monadnock in Fog

What is faith but acquiescence
To those old intractables, space and time?
What is faith but trust

That the unseen mountain
Will waver as the fog lifts, then slowly
Root its ragged hulk to the horizon again,

Or that the hours will bring you back, you
Who have also joined
The Congress of the Invisible?

Yet as I stand in the field
Which lies flat and open, a prelude
To the missing view,

As I look, still stunned, into that
Gleaming abyss where it once stood, that brute
Of a mountain I love,

I'm in the mood
To hold my ground.
Never mind faith, common sense, habit,

I'd stand here until you came back,
Your mass displacing the air between
My arms again. I would wait

Through the frozen midpoint
Of our late-millennial winter,
Until I began to feel my body

Loosen its grip,
And I knew why the martyrs lifted their eyes,
Half-smiling,

As their bodies opened in flames
Like flowers loosening spores.
The air will touch me purely then, the cold

Pour in like raw grace,
Until I no longer wait for you to reappear,
But am with you, my hands

Moving slowly, carefully
Over your sheer face,
Moving down your sides, exploring each crag,

Each slick granite outcrop,
Moving down slowly, down
Into the canyon

Where the brook of spring lies frozen,
Waiting for release,
Touching you there.

First Snow

This slow, meticulous erasure
Leaves nothing of the colors that earth bled
In those weeks of trees going red,
Red-pink, and yellow.

Now the sky seems
An enormous gray overhang—
None of those single, shapely clouds
That browsed through autumn's blue acres.

I can't stop talking about color.
All this white all at once
Seems like some kind of slaughter—
But so lightweight and quiet, I can hardly protest.

Some would find it gorgeous, this
Bleached monopoly. It dwells in the Ideal,
The pure Plato from which all
The other weathers have fallen.

Yet to see the backyard gone from tarnished grass
To something smooth and slick,
Without even the primitive alphabet
Left by a sparrow's meander . . .

This morning, the last of the geese
Pass overhead,
Their *whonk-whonks* cutting through
The leaden clouds.

It's been years since I've wanted to fly,
Imagined my legs fading as I rose, imagined
The earth shrinking to a blue-green curve
As my being

Lifted elsewhere—
Who knows where?
Far from this season, the shapes it stole;
From the beloved shape of any thing.

Eve to Adam, in Retrospect

For awhile, we were riled up,
And all of it inspired by the body, incubate of appetite,
On which the senses hang like fruit.

And didn't we pluck them? Wasn't that
What night was about? Stellar cave of moan and cloud.

I would chart the hours
To and from you; you beckoned and I came.

And weren't there trails of clothes toward the bed?
We rode roughshod
Over that plain, oblivious to the sheeted verge.

And didn't we know what inoperable condition
We had assumed? Desire
Without love, smolder-house without a furnace,
And didn't we burn?

And the moon raked us like coals and brought back the blaze.

The leaves hang in yellow tatters now.
The fields are busy with crows. Still, old darling,
As I walk through this ruined world we built,
Heat for you
Clings to me, dogged as bramble.

The Wood-Burning Stove

You've seen these squat iron monsters,
Their snouts disappearing up chimneys, their hinged mouths
Always ready to be fed—
The inferno I keep
Among flowered pillows, the blackened hunger-room
Right here, in the heart of the house.

Or perhaps itself the heart.

Outside, the news is winter. Everything I loved
Is closed, denuded, frozen, flown south.
And I, just a wall's-worth away from the freeze—

You see why I'm attached to my stove,
Its crackling lingo. When I raise the lid,
It brightens with affection. And when I throw another log on,
Its flames ungirdle the tight-wound rings
Until the sap sizzles. It's a consummation ending
As consummation should, in a spate of smolder and smoke.

The moon arrives on the rug, its beams
As blue and cold as theory. It gives so little,
This winter moon, it floats so high.
Who wouldn't admire such spare expenditure?

But the stove is my mentor:
Fiery, yet contained, raging but formal, the muscular flames
Beating against iron, which does not give but glows,
Remembering its first, molten life,
The acute pleasures of free-flow.

One log more,
One more feast,

And I'll let the flames go from yellow to red.
Swaddled in quilts on the couch, I'll sleep
As the cold draws close, aching
To lie at my side.

Valediction

Your Mozart is not my Mozart anymore.
That hour has passed,
The harmony that thrilled us, the false sun
We warmed to. Your days are yours now
To pile up like dry leaves in your past, from which my past

Has broken off, diverged, gone
Into another woods altogether. No, I cannot make my way over
To you, to touch your face or other parts, not even those whose ache
I can feel at the great distance
That has fallen between us like a world.

I have measured the hours and days since we touched.
Each one healed as I handled it. In them grew this voice, still singing
Out of doubt and longing, a stricken sound.

You are struck from the record. Your hand, absolved
Of my flagrant touch. Dismantle the room
Where we've become marble figures, a white
Sculptured kiss; where we sat listening
To your Mozart, not mine.

To the Curious Reader

I know you want to know
What nights have meant to me, to get the facts.

Whose hand is raised toward whom? Was I really
Capable of all this implies? And what kiss is that,

That sears the last line? Don't ask.
That kiss has been paid for.

The words come long after, to pluck at the dead
And make their report.

What happened
Was more a property of heat than mind,

An undue undressing that shucked virtue off.
But ah, I grow cryptic again.

You want to know
What sin was involved, why I so often speak

Of absolution.
Those absolute certainties I, too, want.

But it's the body that I keep waking to.
Loneliness haunts it

And the face of one who left me behind,
Which corresponds to everything now,

Rather neatly, in fact. In fact,
I think you may be right: I owe you a confession.

Though some things defy recounting in words,
These tiny icons I cherish, with syllables for feet.

By your leave then, dear reader,
I strike a balance between fact and sound.

I leave history
To the boys who write in prose.

Mortal Thoughts

At twelve, a reader of the martyrs' lives,
I imagined my own body likewise
Flayed, starved, boiled, my mouth filled to the brim
With molten lead, my eyes stamped out like fires.

To be a grass: that would be good, I thought.
No pain. And when we got to single-celled,
Spineless breeds in sixth-grade science class
(Timothy H. across the aisle, leering,
Miming kisses), the life of an amoeba
Seemed just fine. It didn't even hurt to think
What brief, orgasmic shudder it would take
To shut such evanescence down.

                              Each morning,
I'd fish my wary prepubescent image
Out of the mirror, thinking with some triumph,
Some desperation, *I'm still here!*

                              I'm *still* here.
And like the saint enamored of the rack
That slowly winds her toward salvation,
I'm tethered to this turning earth
Where love in all its dangerous forms is made.

II. Claudia Poems

The Young Men of Division Street

They lounge around the light post, smoking,
Cool and easeful
As young Olympians. Their bodies are still
A means, not an end, their pickups
Parked on the street
With epithets scrolled above the grilles:

Bat Outa Hell and *Blue Heaven.*

As Claudia walks by, one flashes a grin at her,
And it feels like the cool slap of air
That rises when a shovel
Opens the earth.

Tentatively, she smiles back,
Walks up the stairs to her studio, opens the door,
And faces her blank canvas, the site
Of her next rigorously-composed world—

Imagining herself down there on the street,
Lighting up, feeling what it is to have
A small flame
Near her lips, to slowly
Breathe in smoke, to bring fire
Closer and closer to her body.

Curriculum Vitae

She made her minor reputation
With purely mental fields of color
That she layered on canvas with a broad brush.

Is not, she said to her friends,
Half-drunk in an East Village bar, *the color
Blue enough?*
And ordered another round for the table.

She read the modernists, post- and pre-.
She wore black leather. Hey,
Claudia was hip, no question.

Then came the teaching job. Westfield.
Fields of corn that drove the eye
All the way out to the festering horizon.
I do tractors, the guy at El's Bar told her;
You know, farm kind of stuff. Then, touching
Her jacket, *You sure black's your color?*

She was not.
Her volumes of *Art in Theory,*
Unread, piled up. Between the pages,
She pressed late-August flowers; by fall,
They grew as transparent as wisdom.

One morning, she sat in her studio,
Facing a marigold stuck in a vase.
Took in the goldness, the feathery leaves.

The flower's garlicky musk rose toward her;
The generosity of it all
Weighed in.

She picked up a brush,
And, like a lover trying to satisfy
The beloved and her own rash hunger,

She began to render,
From the Latin *rendere*, "to give back."

The Good Fortune of Others

As she walks down the hall in her usual flurry,
Claudia hears her name—

It's her sculptor friend, calling out
From her studio:

Hey Claudia, I just had a day
When everything I touched turned to gold.

Claudia backs up three steps,
Pokes her head in the door,

Gives her the thumbs-up sign and smiles,
Amazed at the ease of some people.

Freeze them at any moment, snap their pictures,
And they're snug in the center of some universe

She's never visited, she who can
Hardly take a step without pausing to reconsider:

Do the wash?
Fall in love?

All the while, her Teacher's voice in her head,
Trying to cut through the static:

Remember, my dear, the Greeks said the prize
Was not happiness, but contentment.

Calla Lily Studies

Keeping her eyes on the flower,
She tracks the stem's ascent
With a slow green stroke that arrives in
The painting's small heaven.

There, switching brushes,
She opens the milky cup,
Following each curve of the blossom up, out
To where it curls —

Feels the insistence of that edge. Tries to render it
With a gray-blue like smoke, a stroke
That angles down,
Lifts —

The third time, she gets it right. In the fourth,
Takes on the fluted profile,

And so on, until, on the floor around her,
Lilies drift up, unfold, their whites
Verging on inflorescence.

Dizzy from the spotlight's heat,
A streak of green
Fading on her brow, she breathes, *One more:*

A straight-on view, the powdered pistil
Lifting from the lily's throat, the painting's heart,
A final protuberance
Of earth's untutored darkness and her own strong will.

Brush tip to pistil tip, she holds —
The studio mazed with light, the air flowering
With the stink of cadmium yellow.

Self-Portrait as Woman Posed
on Flowered Couch

She thought her education would come
All at once, as it did
For Saul, lucky boy, trailed by lightning
Until the right moment,
Crawling out from under his horse
With a new name and obsession.

But daily the weather comes around,
And he who claims to love her
Is still there in the morning,
Buttering toast,
Calling her yet
Another nonsensical name.

She imagined the battles of the soul
Fought out
In the old high style, leaving her
Dappled with virtue.

But she finds that she's infected
With a mild self-love;
She's the would-be martyr
Who dreams of the executioner's knife
And wakes praising heathen gods
In her safe bed.

What will educate her
To the mirror and the clock,
All those exigencies?

Like a flower,
She colors in the moment.

Meanwhile, the anger of God
Waits in the cupboards, ready to fill the house,
Upbraiding the meek
Philodendron, astonishing
The dust on the sills.

En Route

Her plane leaves at six.
They sit at an early supper, her mother getting up
To add to the potatoes, to cook more peas.

One can never have enough vegetables,
She says to no one in particular, as Claudia's father
Holds forth on classical physics.

Now there was a science, he says. *Everything fit,*
Neatly as clockwork. That was their metaphor,
You know.

Claudia nods. *More salad?* her mother intervenes,
And she nods again, still there in the middle,
Her hands shaped like her mother's, with the same
Nervous flutter of unmet need; her will
As fierce as the will her father wields. *Look up!*

He once said, showing her the night sky. *All that, mine,*
And just for the looking.
Sight was such a pleasure to him,
And distance, also.

Now she's in the foyer,
Suitcase in hand. Her mother
Slips a sandwich in her purse: *The trip is so long,*
She says. Her father offers his cheek for a kiss,
And she plants it carefully, in the spot
Where she's left her kisses for years.

Beyond them, the living room
Is scattered with pools of lamplight.
The botanical prints she stared at as a child
Still there on the walls, their flowers drawn
With stupefying exactness:

Each dot of dew on a petal
Reflecting an invisible sun, each leaf observed
With some love or fear that could not leave
One serration unrecorded.

How she loved and feared that vision!
Like God's, it took the world whole,
With no thing left to the imagination.

Good-bye, she says to her parents, to the living room,
To all those tiny, perfect drops of dew.
She opens the door:

The cab waits in the driveway.
The sky is charged with her father's stars.

A sandwich in her purse, she will
Fly through them, and find her way beyond home.

Red Light, Roma

Fiats in silver-blue clouds of exhaust
Stream past, headed toward
The fraying stones of the Coliseum.

She opens her map and sighs.
Not a spot here left unmarked, not the site
Of a temple, forum, gallows, vision.

A few steps more, and she's up
To her neck
In someone else's history again —

She'll have to wade through,
Her own life
Like a shambles on a string,

A backwater ditty
That only she knows.
She wants to enlarge,

Appropriate crowns,
Undo the crowd with a miracle!
Or at least,

To warrant stature
As a minor figure, to earn one graffito
In a major city —

Claudia lives on!

The light goes green, but Claudia's
Still on her curb, feeling her heart
Ticking in her chest.

Like Caesar on his hill in Gaul
She stands,
Unnerved by that mild tempo.

Il Monte

Every morning it floats
Above the city's ragged horizon:
Hazy, like a face viewed through steam.

Later, cleared, it glares down, chilly as pewter.

Claudia takes a sip of her coffee,
Trying to shake the funny little feeling
That this cold far-offness, this rigid light
Is the irate God of her childhood come back to haunt her.

And he is
Appalled at how she's taken to this city
Where fountain nymphs loll
Above rusting pennies, their marble garments slipping off
In the wanton spray. The grocer on the corner
Spends an hour stacking his oranges, and why?
E bella, he says to her, shrugging. There are,
Moreover, more Venuses per capita here than in any town
Either side of the Mississippi.
She's counted twelve so far. Some without arms,
Some without heads.
But there's no mistaking that famous torso.

Slowly,
In spite of herself,
She slows down. Buys an orange,
Then two lemons, to put on the table next to her bed.
And why?

Because they're beautiful.

That very afternoon,
She smiles at a stranger across the café,
Turns to the waiter, orders one more Campari—

What next
For the Puritans' daughter, adrift
Among cobbled *vicoli*, the scent of flowers
Stippling the heat,
The canaries in windows warbling her deeper
Into the flesh-tinted dusk?

Later, wandering alone up the side
Of the Gianicolo Hill,
She pauses to take in the view—
Purpling domes, roofs fading out
To where the mountain, an adamant red, rises up.

It has seen her. It has read her heart.

Suddenly feeling an old-fashioned panic,
Claudia steps back
To stand in the darker dark of the palms.

The Imperial Forum

Headless vestals on moldering pedestals,
Pillars for a temple *in absentia,*
An arch that ends midcurve:

She follows its broken trajectory
Back to Westfield, those autumn afternoons
When the light poured in
Through pure gold leaves—

How that light
Gave their bodies a patina.

Amorous congestions on the bed,
Illusions of touch!
She thought that they had arrived beyond
History's landscape,
The usual mistake of the passionate.

Gazing into the Roman sky
Bleached pastel-blue by the sun,
Claudia feels something in her lean, fall,
Break into dust—

Oh love
That the wind lifts and carries now
Toward the provinces.

The Sistine Chapel

Why, I do believe
He was the greatest
Artist of all time:

American, in a southern accent.

It's the guy next to her, craning his neck back
To take it all in, while Claudia, exhausted
By this universe
Of fake lunettes and dour sibyls,
Brings her head down and rubs her eyes.

Of course, she says,
He was great—

And Caravaggio, hot-shot
Of shadow and light,
Bernini with his raptured Teresa, Angelico
Who made Saint Stephen beam
Shyly in his technicolor robes.

And she?

Merest Claudia, *americana,*
Who in the calm of the Roman night
Hears the pickups of Westfield backfire through her dreams—?

Silenzio! barks the mustached guard.

The secular hum fades.
Claudia looks skyward: there's Adam,
Lounging on our earthly turf
With the sweet calm look of the newly made,

And God
Leaning from his cloud to install Adam's soul—
The Artist, giddy with faith in his materials.

Back to the Mega-Store

Her continental *brio* starts to fade
Somewhere between the canned soup aisle
And the freezer case of New World peas.

Outside, the fields beyond the parking lot
Are still for sale, still keeping the view
Open to the west.

A sack of groceries in each arm, she scans
That huge, available, bereft horizon,
Remembering the Puritan's cry:

Waste and howling wilderness
Far off from heaven's light.

Then Whitman, centuries later, louder singing:

Far swooping elbow'd earth . . .
Smile, for your lover comes.

Nightmare

Men in hoods. Men asking her
Where she'd like to be hit:

She must choose. She must
Waken, and she does with a start—

Moonlight sheathing the dresser.
The armoire hulking in shadow.

She's the only thing
Alive in the room,

And right now,
That's no consolation.

She feels the air move into her chest.
She imagines her bones,

So many,
So close to the surface.

She grows aware of all the moist
And delicate ways in, thinking

As long as she's got this body,
She'll never be safe.

Meditation, Mid-December

The neighbor's daughter has died.

The phone rings: her sculptor friend.
Can't come tonight,
Work to do.

Me too, Claudia says, knowing her work
Is to sit at this window, watching the snow
Pile up and up, to breathe
In winter's accumulating silence.

Childhood was the first season.
Then came that flicker, deep in her body.

She wanted to speak of it.

Wanted to find, as well, someone who knew
That speech
Was just the beginning, that touch
Might diffuse her into another element.

—All this in the soul
Of an impossibly tall, thin girl
Whose black-rimmed glasses
Were so thick they left
Small, red dents on her nose.

Oh, the unlikely tabernacles of Eros!

If she could hold that child she had been,
She would tell her
That the clamoring in her body
Would find release, that the bones in her face
Would sort themselves out,
Until, under some lights, in certain mirrors,

She would appear
Almost beautiful . . .

Somewhere in Westfield,
In a cool and unlit room,
Lies the body of that young woman.

Last fall, Claudia watched as she
Sashayed down the street,
Holding hands with a guy. Her lips
Were outrageously red; her face shone
With new knowledge.

Now, Claudia says to the snow,
Now, she knows everything.

The house of the bereaved
Blazes out in the dusk.

On a branch of the maple before her,
A sparrow appears and quivers.
A skirmish of wings, a blurred diagonal,
And it is gone, leaving to Claudia
The branch's twisted shape,
A flourish of calligraphy on cold gray air.

It makes the character for something,
She is sure,
Either "emptiness" or "wonder"—

The Buddha would say
They are one and the same.

—In memory of Jennifer Bonner

Still Life with Pear

She takes off Dylan, drops in Bach.
Makes coffee, then tries tea. The phone—
Thank God! But it's a wrong number.

She's back at the sink,
Re-washing her brush, trying to get
The last taint of color out—

The canvas on the easel
Still an untroubled beige.
The day going fast.

Her life going. Like her mother's,
A picking up and setting down
And earnest polishing of the silver.

She pauses, the brush still dripping.
I never liked it, her mother said. *Do you?*
Never liked

How they lie on top,
Taking their pleasure, never
Liked it.

She turned toward the window
As Claudia turns now,
Eyes filling with tears.

Slowly she lifts the brush in her hand,
Slowly, examines
The light wooden shaft,

The stiff, sheared-off tip
Smelling faintly of turpentine.
Trusty blade, shining bough, old reliable,

Ready—
The clouds outside shift.
A pear on the still-life table

Lifts from the shadows to show
Its heavily rounded shape, its perfectly
Shameless green.

Out of Love

She stands in the midst of her canvases,
Wondering at their hothouse flowers,
Their bright, high-key colors.

What were *these* all about?

Something in her whispers *Loss* —

Ongoing and simple. Not just of him, who once
Darkened her doorways,
A smile wavering on his lips.

She turns to the still-life table
Cluttered with rocks, books, pipe fittings, vases,
All flea-market finds,

All, just hours back, almost rhapsodic
In morning sun, now
A late-Braquean mass of glinting and shade.

This is her light now, this, her signature,
Along with a harder looking,
The cool, dry-eyed gaze

Of one who has stood waist-deep in water,
Arms folded, the shore a few yards behind;

Who has felt each oncoming wave break on her body,
An invitation from the distant glitter;

Who has yet remained standing, looking out, saying
No, firmly and tenderly to the deep water, *Not yet.*

A Dialogue in the Park

She leans back on the bench and closes her eyes,
The fountain making its happy watery sound.

May I? Startled,
She looks up. His head looms between her
And the blue, blue Westfield sky:

The guy from the bar. Nice voice.
And something else that she sees in his eyes
As he smiles and points to the empty bench beside her:

The dim shine
Of the freighted heart.

She feels her own call out *Comrade,*
Kindred spirit.

But hasn't she finally gotten
Her palette in order, darks to lights?
That other man's socks finally out of her wash?

She's in love
With her latest canvas, little homemade world
Where she decides what recedes
And what steadies in the foreground.

Go lightly, she says to herself,
Saying aloud,
I'm sorry, this is not a good time—

Feeling something in her close, and something open.

Among Cows

The field rolls with mist.

She approaches the herd, avoiding
The narrow tarnished pond,
The ashy piles of dried dung.

She comes not to feed them, as some do.
Not to lead them off to slaughter.

Nor with love, really.

If she were asked to define her mission here,
She would say that she attends upon
Something admittedly as suspect as the visible.

Gauging a safe distance,
She sets down her canvas stool,
Unpacks the thick, soft brushes,
Makes a wash of water and ink.

A few in the herd look up and contemplate her,
Their grass-filled mouths moving.
Then one slowly detaches itself
And with a sumptuous motion,
Ambles off to one side,

Stops,
Turns its head, and poses
With all the nonchalance
Of an Aphrodite, certain of the beauty
Of her white belly and throat.

They look at one another a long time,
Claudia and this cow.

The Pleasures of Perspective

She's about to leave the gallery,
Its faded walls and dirty skylight,
When a small Dutch landscape near the door
Catches her eye.

Here, at last, a world run by rules!

They insist that the castle, being closer,
Necessarily dwarfs the distant, perfect city,
And the foreground's fisherman
(The calm lines of his back
Suggesting a fisherman's happiness)
Is largest of all.

She could linger near this fisher,
Tossing stones into his black-green lake.
But why not go on?

There are more views beyond this one,
More sails tipped toward home,
And in the overlapping hills, spires point
To a dozen heavens.

There,
Where the river flows toward
A final mountain, where the landscape
Hones to the vanishing point,
She finds the room and hour
Where memory begins:

The windows transfusing
Morning light; the cool floor;
Not even her father risen.

III. Leave of Absence

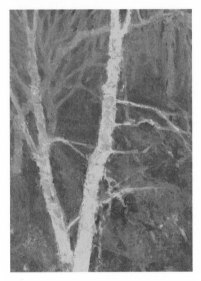

Preface to a Gesture

You know me:
I'm all for putting a rose in the vase,
Long-stemmed or not, red or yellow.

At the drop of a hat, I'll order a trinket
For my neck, my material,
Mortal, lightly-powdered neck—

All this doing and fetching!
I'm in love with the outer world, its sexy
Three dimensions. I've courted the depths
Of mirrors, hoping for a winner,
The smile that could open doors, mouths, stop
The small talk at big parties.

Thee, Vanitas! Whom my good mother
Warned me against; whom our good,
Dead, Puritan forefathers silently condemn
As they grow evermore ashen.

But darling,
It's been one of those days.

And as we sit on the couch, the couch vanishes,
Rose by tapestried rose;
The mirror on the wall becomes
A polished hallway into night.

Now I know what I've always known:

That at the heart of each brick is a pile of dust
As well as the small wind needed
To blow it away;

That faintly penciled on every bone
Are instructions for its undoing
In fire or in sleep.

These, the facts glistening around us
As I turn, face you, reach over.

Elegy in Four Parts

1. Checkup

I haul myself onto the midwife's cot,
Exasperated with my new weight.
I'm tired, I'm in the grip of nausea—
Let's just say the charm of pregnancy

Has worn off. *I'm sure we'll hear something today,*
The midwife croons. I nod and close my eyes.
She pushes up my sweater, spreads the gel,
Then moves a metal thing across my belly,

Picking up the weird, inner-body static,
Pops and cracklings that suddenly clear
Into the beating of your heart, a meter
So skilled that it makes sound itself a story.

The blue fluorescents buzzing, sifting down
The pale light of beatitude, I weep.
The midwife looks at me, alarmed, relieved
When I say *It's so beautiful*—those, your first iambs.

2. The Happiness Psalm

For awhile, we were more than two. We had
Got with child, and life was good:
In every pot, a chicken; in every cloud, a God.
We knew the day that we lay coldly, ash to ash,
Something of us would weigh earth down, yea,
Our protoplasm had found a new frame,
And it fit fine.

Surely, child, you felt our happiness
Through the thin walls of my body.
Surely you knew what we knew for awhile:

The glass filled to the top, the sock
Knitted without error, the ripe wheat golden
Underneath the reaper's rising blade.

3. The Third Stage of Grief

Coming home from the hospital,
I find spring is up
And running full force,

The lilacs next to the bed
Smelling almost too sweet, as if
Trying to redress an imbalance.

Of which world am I?
That of the small box on the dresser,
With its plastic bag of ashes, light as silt?

Or that of these raw lavenders,
Trees scorched with blossoms, evening horizons
Done up in clear pastels?

I, forced to take up
The days, the weeks, the months
That you refused to enter.

4. The Scattering of Ashes

I sing of your light disappearance,
Of a shadow earth never bore.
I am glad for all you'll never weep for,
The loneliness you won't feel,
The long, empty nights on land. But

Where are you now? What do you know?

We gave you to the Atlantic,
What little of you we had—
Substance of a small wind, heat dispensed
When the hand plays a grace note—

You were that light,
Dear, that light.

And how will the sea learn to hold you,
Small thing whom my arms held?

I will not forget your face,
No, I keep its memory near:
You had the calm look of the late sleeper,
Sleeping your way back
Through summer to spring,
Back to the hour of your birth,
Further back
To the night our lovemaking woke you,
The November wind
Hurling against the house.

Stay there, still safe, nothing more
Than a kiss made in the dark, a heart
Just beginning to beat faster.

To the Peony

Your brazen petals weigh on the bush
Until the thin stalk swoons and brings you
Like a tight-laced Victorian to the ground. Even so,
From the dust, you emit your airs—

There's no inflection of petal in you,
No nuance of leaf
Not designed to take away the breath of lesser beings,
Like this bee that just droned by, breaking your heart.

Peony, I'm in nature for a long time,
I have a past, a future, too, and they're both trouble.

But you, you make your pink point
In a week, put forth what you know
Before the heat of June sets in and you
Give up your ghost—

Now, what kind of dainty might that ghost be?

It's the shade of your shade,
The pedigree of pale,
Ding-an-sich of cheap perfume fluttering
Through the late spring portal where they all go,
The former luminaries of this dark earth.

To the Tiger in the Shriners' Parade, Hanover, N.H.

Where have you come from? How dark is your cage?
And what do you think of the local maples,
The big, square green cut with wide paths,
The white church where a very nice God is worshipped?

I'd like to see you, big-pawed guy, to feed you meat.
I'd applaud when you opened your mouth and yawned,
When you showed your teeth and your hot pink tongue—
But I'm sick, I'm in bed on damp cotton sheets,
Drinking tea made from herbs and flowers.

I sleep. I waken, and the sound of faint applause is gone;
Gone, the complaining flutes.

Perhaps you hear the wheeze of wind in maples,
As I do. Perhaps you look out and see our small cache of stars,
Alarmingly far off. What fury they breed in us,
Tiger-boy, those pin-dots, whose light
Beats like drums through the summer-fevered air.

A Mourning Dove in New York City

Waking, I hear its cryptic trill
And I'm back twenty years, in bed
At my grandmother's house, on sheets
Scarred by her mending.

Downstairs, the clock chimes.
My grandmother's steps begin to trace
The choreography of breakfast-making.
I hear my mother's voice, then
Her second-generation laughter.

I slip from the bed.
The floor is cold, the stairs down
Dangerously steep. I waver at the top of them,
Adrift in the scent of coffee . . .

A renter wakes there this morning.
The china cups: sold. As for the clock—
Someone has it who cannot translate
Its hourly lament for the deep,
Aromatic couch, the faint edge
Of lace doily shining.

The cry of the mourning dove rises
Over a small midwestern town,
Over the prairie churning out
Wheat and flowers, over those sheets,
Wherever they are, their stitches still locked
In small, endless embraces,

And wakens me from an older sleep, desiring
To be at table between two large, female bodies,
Watching the morning sun
Set dime store glasses afire.

For a Friend Since Youth

Sixteen years old and bored,
We damned the world
And at 2 A.M. took your slipshod Chevy
To the road.

Even at high speed,
The air flowing through the windows
Was calm and sweet with summer.

As you rounded a curve, laughing,
I imagined the brakes singing like crazed seraphim,
Our bodies breaking through the windshield
As if it were the surface
Of the smooth black lake we swam in.
I closed my eyes, shivering
At that sudden, pleasurable chill.

How careful I've become with my life.

Over tea today,
We spoke of the city, glittering and dangerous;
Of my nuclear dreams;

Of those cells in your body the doctors call
"Precancerous," which you
Laugh off, your eyes
Still that rare light green,
Your head massed with the curls
That once made boys' fingers itch
For new knowledge.

Tonight, 2:03 on my digital,
I'm wakened by an explosion
Somewhere north of 125th,

The breakers of sound
Washing massively through our courtyard.
I sit up, panicky, thinking, *Dear God,*
We've blown the damn world up.

But the wall-crippling heat, the light that blinds
With the belligerence of holiness
Does not come.

Then I remember your face
As it looked today, the candle's flames
Dimming on your pure cheeks—

You, my rabbit's foot, my charm,
You are tinder;
Like the earth, you are the perishable
Source of grace, still with me

As sirens in the hills of Harlem
Raise and twine their distant keen.

After the Stillbirth, Autumn

Our old maple diminishes as it rises,
The branches growing thinner, more delicate,
As if leery of scratching October's
Porcelain blues. A leaf or two
Still clings to those outmost twiggy places,
Like the flames that burned in Rome long after
The barbarians' ravages—

No, that's bad. Like the flags on the rigging
Of an abandoned ship—

You see, I have lots of time for metaphor,
A low-level fever heating my face, the long, light drunk
Of exhaustion upon me.

Sad and drowsy flesh of mine,
What should I make of you? The doctor says
It's the ganglia, those tiny trees in the brain:
They're worn down, poor nerves. Their endings
Throb with the memory of the child's face,
Whose eyes will not open, no matter what song I sing.

The world's in shambles:
Leaf hordes rattling down the street, a late-shift wind
Scourging the clouds.

The season of absence is upon us
And I have yet to learn what my old maple knows—
How to draw the heart-heat to an inner ring
Where it will glow moltenly all winter,
Like jars of provisions set by.

An Imaginary Tapestry

Bushes, flowers, birds half-camouflaged by leaves,
Their wings flickering like the needle's motion
As it dipped in and out: all of this frames
The clearing, where a peasant couple
Dances mirthfully, their hands clasped above them,
Their cheeks rounded by clusters of reddish knots
That burn with the blood risen hotly
From their invisible tapestried hearts.

Move back a step, and it comes into view:
A single gold thread running through midway up,
A clear-belled note. It smites like the shrill
Voice of conscience. Inorganic,
Incongruous, it remains on the surface,
Glinting and vaguely perverse. A slip-up,
Perhaps? But it's gold, and so obvious.

See how the eye returns to it, how
The mind in its study grows more formal,
Ready to forsake the dancing couple,
The birds in the bush, the castle floating
On a background hill, its airy turrets
Lost in a bevy of threadbare clouds.

Now it is all that you see. See how
It glitters, grows irresistible in this
Otherwise beautifully faded world.

To Helen, from Moose Island, Maine

Having lost the precision of your body,
You seem monumental
As these moving messes of water and fleshy clouds.

So I fall back on history, remembering
How I crooned over your small shape. You were
Like a bibelot brought across deserts and mountains,
Finely worked, each detail intact—
A signature piece, my dear, I didn't need the magnifier
To see that—
Only the mechanism of breath curiously stalled.

Meanwhile, the doctors running in with blood,
Sacks of it, their white coats flapping comically.

I was interested only in you, your eyes
Fixed forever on something beyond me. What was it
That had caught your attention?
I turned and looked. Stared,
But could not see it. Then the anesthesia
Flooded me, inking you out.

Looking now from this wind-wracked point
To a bay full of islands steaming in mist,
I dwindle to something historical, knickknack of earth,
Shoofly in the golden rooms of time.

Now, I appreciate your pluck—
You, who did not turn back
Once it had opened before you, the difficult sea
That you are still crossing alone.

Fra Angelico's *Annunciation,* Convent of San Marco

If it weren't for the angel's wings—
Always a giveaway—
You might mistake these two for sisters,

Their robes stained
From the same palette of ruddiness,
Their hair swept off their faces, falling
In similar gold curls.

Yet they keep their distance,
As does Dominic, the saint in the yard,
Who from the Renaissance
Looks on shyly,
His hands held formally in prayer,
His black and white habit austere
Next to the angel's wings,
The venial pink that lingers,
Not yet redeemed, in Mary's cheek.

Probably his prayerful stance
Is apropos: how often, after all,
Are we promised saviors?

Still, I can't help but wish
That the saint had been braver,
Had reached out and fingered those wings—
Oh, just
Inches away!

And had let us know
What an angel's made of.

After the Old Testament Lecture, Taking the Shortcut Home

Hearing a sudden rush of wings
As something above me, startled
By my approach, lifts
Into ruffled flight,

I cry out
For the both of us, stumble off the path
And into a bush
Like a nervous slapstick comic—

The woods still unbrightened by snow,
The sky above me moonless,
My flashlight
Home on the shelf.

Think!
I say to myself, my old fear
Of darkness rising,
Think!

And stagger to my feet,
Conjuring the image
Of our mild Carmelite monk,
One finger raised
In a preacherly gesture, the other
Poised on his printout.

Hessed,
He told us, *a word the Greeks
Translated "grace,"
In Hebrew means something more like
"Compassion."*

Something creaks above me.
I stiffen
And slowly look up.
A pine's shaggy point heaves
From star to star.

Wind, I say aloud, relieved,
Then continue staring
Into night's overgrown
Seedbed of dark.

Why wind?
I think. Why not translate
Whatever it was that just made its way
Through the still-swaying
Pitch of this pine

As not wind,
And not grace,
But *hessed*,

Compassion breathed
By something that knows what it is to walk
Through woods like these,

On a path unlit, on a night moonless,
Before the first
Great snows of December have fallen.

The Lighthouses Are Automated

Let the keepers sleep tonight. Let the goat
Get in the garden. Let old men fall
To the subway tracks, rain forests vanish,
The hole in the ozone soundlessly widen
Like a hymenal tear at the pole.

We have made our golden age on the cliffs
Where they stand, their meters fingering dusk
As it thickens, as it bears down on us
With its neoclassical strictness.
Then current thrills up each cabled spine
And a beam of light shoots out, as round and pure
As the fabled columns of Corinth.

Nothing else changes: the sea goes on storming,
The fish stream down into ancient shoals,
Their scales in the dimness gleaming faintly,
Like the blood as it moves toward the heart.

Winter Morning with Crow

At the first stroke of sunlight you're at it,
Haranguing me with your vivid
Monosyllabic. You land and strut in the street,
Tut's heir, or Napoleon's—

I'll bet
You would have taken Russia.

And let's face it:
This is your season. You like
All this glitter, the ice stretched
Like thin buffed skins on the walks, the trees'
Bare branches paring the wan blue sky—

There's no better perch
To show you off, and, of course,
There's nothing you like better
Than to be seen, unless
It's to be heard, which pleasure you indulge now,
Cawing and cawing.

At my desk, feeling my 8 A.M. longing
For something endurable,
I put a few words together,
Try to close truth in a chime.

I look up:

You're there, head cocked, looking back,
The feathery given, the bird-shaped dark
Which deforms into flight.

Comrade, how do you leave me?

With a shattered calm,
The maple branch still shaking
As if with a terminal tremor,
And one black feather searing
My tidy backyard stretch of snow.

A Freighter in Eastport

It arrives in rain, a big, gray hulk
Ghosting through the harbor's misty foyer
To shudder against our pier, and hold.
And then its horn exhorts us. How deeply
It speaks the single thought
Of a ship tethered to a village.

Why has it come to upstage us, to unknit our week?
We'd hardly given thought beyond the local
Trees and stars. Now sailors roam the streets in pairs,
Exchanging buttery vowels. They seem like our men.
But I can't help but notice their hands,
So sensitive, their delicate mouths . . .

How *is* joy practiced elsewhere? What wind instrument is played?
Who lies in wait, the woman or the man? And when do they bloom,
The flowers of those other, milder arcadias?

At midnight, I walk to the pier to touch it,
I've become that bold. I want to be sure
That it's real, no, I want to be cured of it, to make it
Just a steel thing attached to us like a canker,
Eating a forest's worth of lumber
Before steaming home to Ecuador.
Its side curves up and away, like a planet's.
I run one finger along its flank, taking in
The bumps and cracks, the rough caress of rusted paint,
The sour sea-smell.

Sometime in the night, it slips away
Without so much as an adios.

But it leaves behind its trail, sea-bright, penetrating
Our giddy horizon.

Leave of Absence

Today it seems preposterous
To have hauled it this far,
This heart—

Like Hannibal going over the Alps—

Wasn't there a way to do
With less baggage?

These views, thank goodness,
Are working their tonic, these strangers
Bring back the pleasures of strangeness,

And after all those months,
Those relentless Novembers,

The afternoon sun pours down so abundantly
That the voices around me expire
Mid-air, the tables and flowers fade—

I'm just trying to take in the sight
Of a birdbath a few feet away,
Sunk at an angle in the yard.

It wants cleaning.

But look
How wind troubles its water
To a superficial beauty.

How it then calms and clears.

See those shadows at the bottom,
How they burn now, now shift, now grow
Utterly still,
Like the mind at work in the world.

Notes

page 43: The Puritan poet quoted is Michael Wigglesworth (1631–1705); the lines in the poem appear in two different places in "God's Controversy with New-England" (1662). Note that the word "heavens" appears in the original without the possessive apostrophe. The lines from Whitman are from "Song of Myself," section 21.

page 52: The details of the poem are based in part on the painting *Landscape with Castle,* by Jacob Grimmer. The work is dated 1592.

About the Author

A native of St. Paul, Clare Rossini is an assistant professor of English at Carleton College in Northfield, Minnesota, and a member of the faculty at Vermont College's low-residency MFA program. She completed her BA at the College of St. Benedict, before taking an MFA at the University of Iowa and a PhD at Columbia University, where she won the Bennett Cerf Award for Poetry and an Academy of American Poets Prize. Among her publications are poems in *Poetry*, *The Kenyon Review*, and *The Best American Poetry* 1997.

About the Book

Winter Morning with Crow was designed and typeset on a Macintosh in Quark XPress by Kachergis Book Design of Pittsboro, North Carolina. The typeface, Electra, was designed in 1935 by William Addison Dwiggins. It is a standard book typeface because of its evenness of form and its high legibility. The display type, Hiroshige, was designed by Cynthia Hollandsworth of AlphaOmega Typography, Inc., in 1986. It was originally commissioned for a book of woodblock prints by Japanese artist Ando Hiroshige.

Winter Morning with Crow was printed on 60-pound Writers Natural and bound by McNaughton and Gunn Lithographers, Inc., of Saline, Michigan.